MY VIOLET POETRY BOOK

Where wild things grow

edited by Moira Andrew

Nelson

'For Katherine'

Thomas Nelson and Sons Ltd
Nelson House   Mayfield Road
Walton-on-Thames   Surrey
KT12 5PL   UK

51 York Place
Edinburgh
EH1 3JD   UK

Thomas Nelson (Hong Kong) Ltd
Toppan Building 10/F
22A Westlands Road
Quarry Bay   Hong Kong

Thomas Nelson Australia
102 Dodds Street
South Melbourne
Victoria 3205   Australia

Nelson Canada
1120 Birchmount Road
Scarborough   Ontario
M1K 5G4   Canada

Selection © Moira Andrew 1988
Illustrations © Macmillan Education Ltd 1988

First published by Macmillan Education Ltd 1988
ISBN 0-333-46570-9

This edition published by Thomas Nelson and Sons Ltd 1991

ISBN 0-17-400588-1
NPN 9 8 7 6 5 4 3 2

Printed in Hong Kong

Acknowledgements

The editor and publishers wish to thank the following who have kindly given permission for the use of copyright material:

The Bodley Head for 'Hi, Coconut' from *I Din Do Nuttin* by John Agard; Iain Crichton Smith for 'Robin' from *A Very First Poetry Book* ed. John Foster, Oxford University Press, 1984; Edna Eglinton for 'Come and Explore My Garden'; John Fairfax for 'Over The Moon'; Aileen Fisher for 'Grass'; John Foster for 'I thought' and 'When the wind blows'. Copyright © 1988 John Foster; Theresa Heine for 'The East Wind and the Sun'; Michael Henry for 'Mumps Medicine'; Hodder and Stoughton (Australia) Pty Ltd. for 'Popcorn' from *Popcorn and Porcupines* by Gordon Winch, 1984; Jean Kenward for 'Icicle Joe'; Brian Levison for 'Christmas Eve' and 'Recipe for a Happy New Year'; Judith Nicholls for 'Chicken Pox' and 'Days of the Week'; Grace Nichols for 'Look' from *I like that stuff* ed. Morag Styles, Cambridge University Press, 1984 and 'Have a Mango' from *You'll love this stuff* ed. Morag Styles, Cambridge University Press, 1986; Ian McMillan and Martyn Wiley for 'Me and Bully Bill'; Macmillan Publishing Company for 'Dragon Smoke' from *I Feel the Same Way* by Lilian Moore, Atheneum Press. Copyright © 1967 Lilian Moore; Wes Magee for 'The Classroom Circle of Friends' and 'Are you ready?' from *Calling, Calling,* Cambridge University Press; Penguin Books Ltd. for 'Winter Morning' from *Custard and Company* by Ogden Nash, selected by Quentin Blake, Kestrel Books, 1979. Copyright © 1979 by the Estate of Ogden Nash and Quentin Blake; Marian Reiner on behalf of the author for 'Yellow Weed' from *Little Racoon and Poems from the Woods* by Lilian Moore. Copyright © 1975 by Lilian Moore; John Rice for 'Apple Jingle, Japple Angle' from *Rockets and Quasars*. Copyright © John Rice 1984; Sheila Simmons for 'The Old Man In The Park'; Ian Souter for 'In The Water'; Mrs. A. M. Walsh for 'The Christmas Tree' by John Walsh from *Poets in Hand* ed. Anne Harvey, Puffin Books, 1985; J. Walsh for 'Eats'.

Every effort has been made to trace all the copyright holders but if any have been inadvertently overlooked the publishers will be pleased to make the necessary arrangement at the first opportunity.

Illustrations by: Val Biro pp 44/45; Francis Blake pp 36/37; Kim Blundell pp 18, 48; Helen Clipson pp 24/25; Barbara Glebska pp 30/31; Anna Hancock pp 28/29, 38/39, 48; Helen Herbert pp 10/11; Julie Hughes pp 16/17, 48; John Lobban pp 20/21; Pat Nessling pp 8/9; Nina O'Connell pp 22/23, 40/41; Mark Peppe pp 12/13, 34/35; Maggie Read pp 32/33, 46; Margaret Sherry pp 6/7, 47, cover; Steve Smallman pp 14/15, 42/43, 46; Ursula Sieger pp 26/27; Joyce Smith pp 4/5.

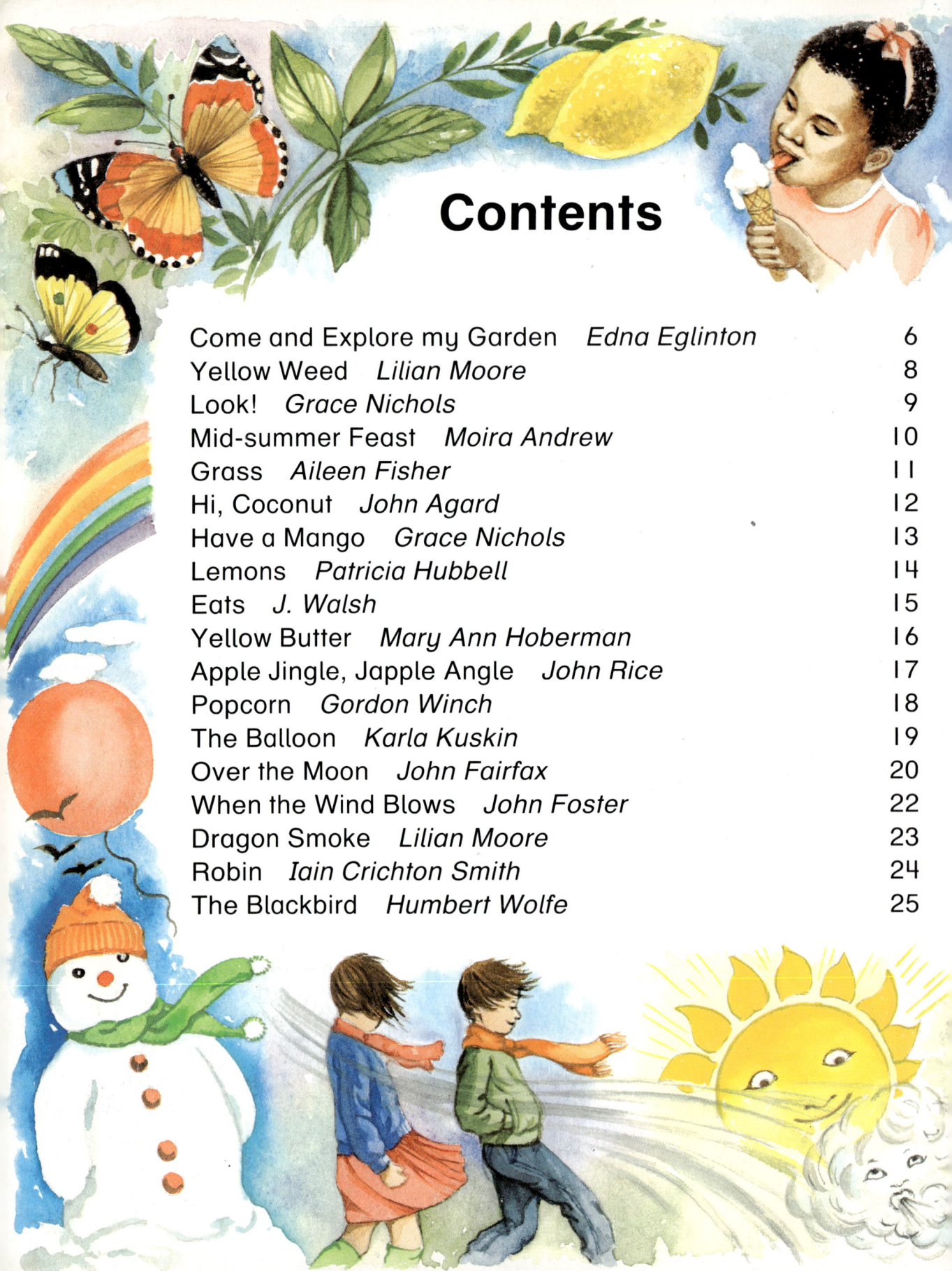

Contents

Come and Explore my Garden

Janet has a garden
That is tidy and neat
With a border of lupins
Beside a garden seat.
Her raspberry canes and cabbages
Stand upright in a row,
But I have a garden
Where wild things grow.

There are buttercups and butterflies
And beetles with green wings,
And tangly brambly bushes
Where the chaffinch sings.
I've seen a hedgehog
Trundling to and fro
At the bottom of my garden
Where the wild things grow.

In Janet's tidy garden
We mustn't run about
Or somersault across the lawn
Or skip or jump or shout
Or crawl about exploring
Or pick the flowers, and so
I'm glad I've got a garden
Where wild things grow.

by Edna Eglinton

Yellow Weed

How did you get here,
weed?
Who brought your seed?

Did it lift
on the wind and
sail
and drift
from a far and yellow
field?

Was your seed a
burr,
a sticky burr that
clung to a
fox's
furry tail?

Did it fly with a
bird
who liked to feed
on the tasty
seed
of the yellow
weed?
How did you come?

by Lilian Moore

Look!

Look at the sunlight
shaking patterns
through the trees.

Look at the raindrops
cupped cool green
cassava leaves.

Look at the bananas
turning
nice and fat and ripe.

Look at the watermelon —
how about
a sweet mouth-watering red slice?

by Grace Nichols

9

Mid-summer Feast

Serve a slice of sunshine,
Pass the plate of breeze,
Garnish with a rainbow
As vivid as you please.

RED of oriental poppy
YELLOW of the flag
ORANGE of fiery marigold
BLUE sea-holly's jag
GREEN of summer grass
INDIGO's iris frill
VIOLET cat-faced pansies
Mix them as you will.

Sip the wine of morning dew,
Wash down with gentle rain,
Try a spoon of ice-cool cloud
Before the day hots up again.

by Moira Andrew

Grass

Do you ever think about grass
on the lawns you pass?
The green of it,
the sheen of it,
the after-raining clean of it
when it sparkles like glass?

Do you know what grass is,
those green spears showing
wherever you're going?

Every blade, to be brief,
is a leaf
without a twig, without a bough.
You never thought lawn mowers
went around
clipping leaves off the ground,
did you, now?

by Aileen Fisher

11

Hi, Coconut

Coconut tree
so tall and high
when I look up at yuh
I got to wink up me eye.

Coconut tree
yuh coconut big
like football in the sky.
Drop down one fo me nuh.

If only I could reach yuh
if only I could reach yuh
is sweet water and jelly
straight to me belly.

But right now coconut
yuh deh up so high
I can't reach yuh
I could only tell yuh,
Hi,
Hi, Coconut!

by John Agard

Have a Mango

Have a mango
sweet rainwashed
sunripe mango
that the birds
themselves
woulda pick
if only they
had seen it —
a rosy miracle

Here

take it from mih hand.

by Grace Nichols

13

Lemons

A lemon's a lemony kind of a thing,
It doesn't look sharp and it doesn't look sting,
It looks rather round and it looks rather square,
It looks almost oval, a yellowy pear.
It looks like a waxy old, yellow old pear,
It looks like a pear without any stem,
It doesn't look sharp and it doesn't look sting,
A lemon's a lemony kind of a thing.
But cut it and taste it and touch it with tongue
You'll see where the sharp and the sting have been hiding —
Under the yellow without any warning;
I touch it and touch it again with my tongue,
I like it! I like it! I like to be stung!

by Patricia Hubbell

Eats

'I'm soft' said the jam
'to spread on the bread.'
'I'm hard' said the cheese
'so slice me instead.'

'I'm soft' said the chocolate
'to melt in a jiffy.'
'I'm hard' said the toffee
'and when chewed I am sticky.'

'I'm soft' said the ice-cream
'to cool tongue and lips.'
'I'm hard' said the apple
'but watch out for my pips!'

by J. Walsh

15

Yellow Butter

Yellow butter purple jelly red jam black bread
Spread it thick
Say it quick
Yellow butter purple jelly red jam black bread
Spread it thicker
Say it quicker
Yellow butter purple jelly red jam black bread
Now repeat it
While you eat it
Yellow butter purple jelly red jam black bread
Don't talk with your mouth full!

by Mary Ann Hoberman

QUALITY CONTROL

Apple Jingle, Japple Angle

Pickem Packem
Stickem Stackem
Apples in a Box

Bitem Munchem
Lickem Crunchem
A Pippin and a Cox.

by John Rice

Popcorn

Pop the popcorn
Pop the popcorn
Pop it in the pot.

Pop the popcorn
Pop the popcorn
See the popcorn pop.

Eat the popcorn hot.

by Gordon Winch

18

The Balloon

I went to the park
And I bought a balloon.
It sailed through the sky
Like a large orange moon.
It bumped and it fluttered
And swam with the clouds.
Small birds flew around it
In high chirping crowds.
It bounced and it balanced
And bowed with the breeze.
It skimmed past the leaves
On the tops of the trees.

And then as the day
Started turning to night
I gave a short jump
And I held the string tight
And home we all sailed
Through the darkening sky,
The orange balloon, the small birds
And I.

by Karla Kuskin

Over The Moon

Over the moon
In Katy's balloon
Jonathan went as the pilot.

Tom on his back
Was keeping close track
Waving good-bye with a Mars bar.

The moon turned round
Like a golden pound
Flipped up from David's finger.

Back from the moon
In Katy's balloon
Jonathan still as the pilot.

Balloon hit a lump
Landed with a bump
In the garden by the window.

Heather stood there
With dust in her hair
Having cooked them all five mooncakes.

The trip was a thrill
The moon's there still
Now waiting for you to find her.

by John Fairfax

When the Wind Blows

When the wind blows
Coats flap, scarves flutter.

When the wind blows
Branches groan, leaves mutter.

When the wind blows
Curtains swish, papers scatter.

When the wind blows
Gates creak, dustbins clatter.

When the wind blows
Doors slam, windows rattle.

When the wind blows
Inside is a haven
Outside is a battle.

by John Foster

Dragon Smoke

Breathe and blow
white clouds
      with every puff.
It's cold today,
      cold enough
to see your breath.
Huff!
Breathe dragon smoke
      today!

by Lilian Moore

23

Robin

If on a frosty morning
the robin redbreast calls
his waistcoat red and burning
like a beggar at your walls

throw breadcrumbs on the grass for him
when the ground is hard and still
for in his breast there is a flame
that winter cannot kill.

by Iain Crichton Smith

24

The Blackbird

In the far corner
close by the swings,
every morning
a blackbird sings.

His bill's so yellow,
his coat's so black,
that he makes a fellow
whistle back.

Ann, my daughter,
thinks that he
sings for us two
especially.

by Humbert Wolfe

The Old Man in the Park

The old man's here again today
on his bench by the chestnut tree,
sharing his crumbs
with each sparrow that comes,
letting them land
on his skinny brown hand,
smiling and talking
and nodding his head
at the little brown birds
that are sharing his bread.

by Sheila Simmons

I thought . . .

I thought it was
a hedgehog
but it was only
an old scrubbing brush
half-buried in the snow.

I thought it was
a blackbird
but it was only
some torn black plastic
caught in the branch of a tree.

I thought it was
a butterfly
but it was only
a scrap of paper
whirling about in the wind.

by John Foster

27

Christmas Eve

When Mummy tucked me into bed
She hung the stocking near my head,
And 'Close your eyes and sleep,' she said,
    And shut the door.

Although it's dark my eyes are bright
And I can see without the light;
I'm going to stay awake all night
    To watch who comes.

Listen, I hear the floorboards crack!
It must be Santa with his sack!
A face looms near and then draws back.
      It's only Dad.

Next time I raise my head to peep,
Presents are lying in a heap!
And I haven't even been to sleep!
      How does he do it?

by Brian Levison

The Christmas Tree

They chopped her down in some far wood
A week ago,
Shook from her dark green spikes her load
Of gathered snow.
And brought her home at last, to be
Our Christmas show.

A week she shone, sprinkled with lamps
And fairy frost;
Now with her boughs all stripped, her lights
And spangles lost,
Out in the garden there, leaning
On a broken post,

She sighs gently . . . Can it be
She longs to go
Back to that far-off wood, where green
And wild things grow?
Back to her dark green sisters, standing
In wind and snow?

by John Walsh

Recipe for a Happy New Year

If you want a happy year
   When things go well for you,
Observe this ancient legend
   Which explains what you must do.

In every house you eat mince pies
   — The story is quite clear —
So many happy months you'll have
   Throughout the coming year.

It does not say how many pies
   Or whether cold or hot,
Or whether cream may be allowed
   Or whether it may not.

Now since I'm very anxious
   For the New Year to be good,
I thought I'd pay a call or twelve
   About the neighbourhood.

So if I rattle at your door,
   Don't run away or scream,
But kindly ask me in to share
   Your hot mince pies — with cream!

by Brian Levison

Winter Morning

Winter is the king of showmen,
Turning tree stumps into snowmen
And houses into birthday cakes
And spreading sugar over lakes.
Smooth and clean and frosty white,
The world looks good enough to bite.
That's the season to be young,
Catching snowflakes on your tongue.
Snow is snowy when it's snowing,
I'm sorry it's slushy when it's going.

by Ogden Nash

Icicle Joe

I made a snowman:
Icicle Joe.
The moon shone round him
high and low . . .
the moon shone round him
sides and back —
it gave him a shadow,
purple black.

I made a snowman
white and plump;
a nose he had
like a sugar lump.
The sun shone round him . . .
One bright day
he slumped a little
and he went away.

Vanishing softly
bit by bit
like a lollipop does
when you suck at it,
only a puddle
stayed to show
where I had built him —
Icicle Joe.

by Jean Kenward

The East Wind and the Sun

The East wind blew,
He blew the trees,
He shook the branches,
Trembled leaves.

He brushed the clouds
Across the sky,
He snatched the kites,
Away they fly.

'I'm strong!' he yelled,
'I stamp and roar,
I'll blow the clouds,
I'll make it pour!'

He blew and blew
With all his might,
A gale was blowing
Day and night.

Then soft and still
Behind the clouds
A gleam of gold,
A shining shower.

The sun appeared
So strong and bright,
It filled the sky
With glowing light.

The wind grew frightened,
Lost his roar,
And slowly sank,
And blew no more.

The sun has won
The fight today,
The sun has shone
The wind away.

by Theresa Heine

Days of the Week

Monday's a
  soapy-wash day,
  start-afresh day,
  run-a-mile day,
  find-a-smile day
    to start the week!

Tuesday's a
  dancing-club day,
  be-a-Cub day,
  do-a-sum day,
  have-some-fun day,
    then carry on!

Wednesday's a
  have-a-swim day,
  then-stay-in day,
  spelling-test day,
  change-your-vest day,
    the middle one.

Thursday's a
  visit-Gran day,
  chips-and-spam day,
  sing-a-song day,
  run-along day,
    and one more's done.

Friday's an
　　end-of-school day,
　　play-the-fool day,
　　tea-and-bun day,
　　nearly-Sunday,
　　　the start of fun!

Saturday's a
　　jolly-sunny day,
　　pocket-money day,
　　get-up-late day,
　　time-to-wait day,
　　　when work is done.

Sunday's a
　　time-for-toast day,
　　beef-and-roast day,
　　comes-round-fast day,
　　a first-and-last day,
　　　then start again!

by Judith Nicholls

37

Are you ready?

It's
September
the
Sixth,
the
day
before
school,
we
go
back
tomorrow
and
I
feel
like
a
fool.
I
can't
find
my
bag,
my
ruler,
my
pen.

I
can
hardly
recall
if
I'm
Andy
or
Ken!
I'm
all
of
a
dither,
tomorrow's
a
haze,
the
school
starts
in
hours
and
I'm
in
a
daze.

by Wes Magee

38

The Classroom Circle of Friends

(➤start here)

and I like Anne

Dan likes me ➤ I like Anne

Dee likes Dan   Anne likes John

Titch likes Dee   John likes Mike

Mo likes Titch   Mike likes Ron

Mitch likes Mo   Ron likes Paul

Ray likes Mitch   Paul likes Pam

Bert likes Ray   Pam likes Jack

George likes Bert   Jack likes Sam

Gert likes George   Sam likes Jane

Jock likes Gert   Jane likes Rick

Faye likes Jock   Rick likes Jo

Chris likes Faye   Jo likes Mick

May likes Chris   Mick likes Val

Ken likes May   Val likes Jill

Phil likes Ken   Jill likes Trish

Trish likes Phil

by Wes Magee

Lies

When we are bored
My friend and I
Tell
Lies.

It's a competition: the prize
Is won by the one
Whose lies
Are the bigger size.

We really do:
that's true.
But there isn't a prize:
That's lies.

by Kit Wright

Me and Bully Bill

I didn't mean to smile
when Bill fell over the stile
it just
appeared.

I didn't mean to grin
when Bill fell in the bin
it just
began.

I didn't mean to laugh
when Bill slipped in the bath
it just
burst.

And I didn't mean to cry
when Bill hit me in the eye
it just
came out.

by Martyn Wiley
and Ian McMillan

41

Chicken Pox

No school, no sums,
no writing, no P.E.,
no Mrs. Lee
calling the register
and wondering where is Sue,
shouting at Tim for being late,
then giving us words to do.
No 'Button up and out to play!'
no friends today —
just mum and me
and lots and *lots*
of sticky calamine
and cottonwool
and
b^ri_gh_t r^ed s_po^ts!

by Judith Nicholls

Mumps Medicine

Hi Bonnie bye Bonnie
I've got the mumps
so can't play today
come again tomorrow.

Been to see the doctor
says to fetch me some medicine
mumps medicine
for those horrid little lumps
and bumps
swelling into humps.

So, hi Bonnie bye Bonnie
can't play today
cause I've got the mumps
hi Bonnie bye Bonnie
I've got the mumps.

by Michael Henry

In the Water

I asked Mum,
If I could paddle in the water.
In fact,
I asked Mum,
VERY NICELY,
If I could paddle in the water.
She said, 'Er well,
NO!'
I said,
'Oh GO ON.
You let David,
Look at him in the water,
He looks like he's on fire.
Mind you, he's in the right place if he were!'
She said, 'Er well,
NO!'
I said,
'What's the point of coming to the seaside,
If I can't jump in the water?
I'll be ever so careful, Mum.
It's not as though I'll harm the water, please?'
She said, 'Er well,
NO! — But she did hesitate.

Now I'd listened very carefully to Mum,
I had!
And I'd thought about everything she'd said,
I had!
But when she wasn't looking,
I tippy-toed down to the water's edge
And I

J^UM_PE^D ^IN Y^{AH}O_O!

And I danced in the water,
And I pranced in the water,
And I sploshed in the water,
And I sloshed in the water,
And I slurped in the water,
And I even burped in the water.
And then it was time to GO.
So I pulled up my socks,
And walked out of the water,
Wearing my brand new,
Bought by Mum,
Y-ESTERDAY,
Shoes!

by Ian Souter

45

Index of First Lines

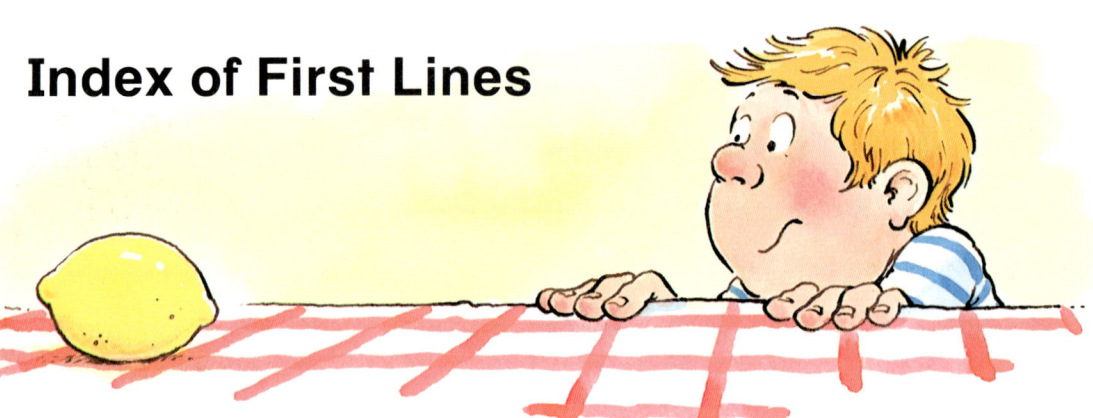

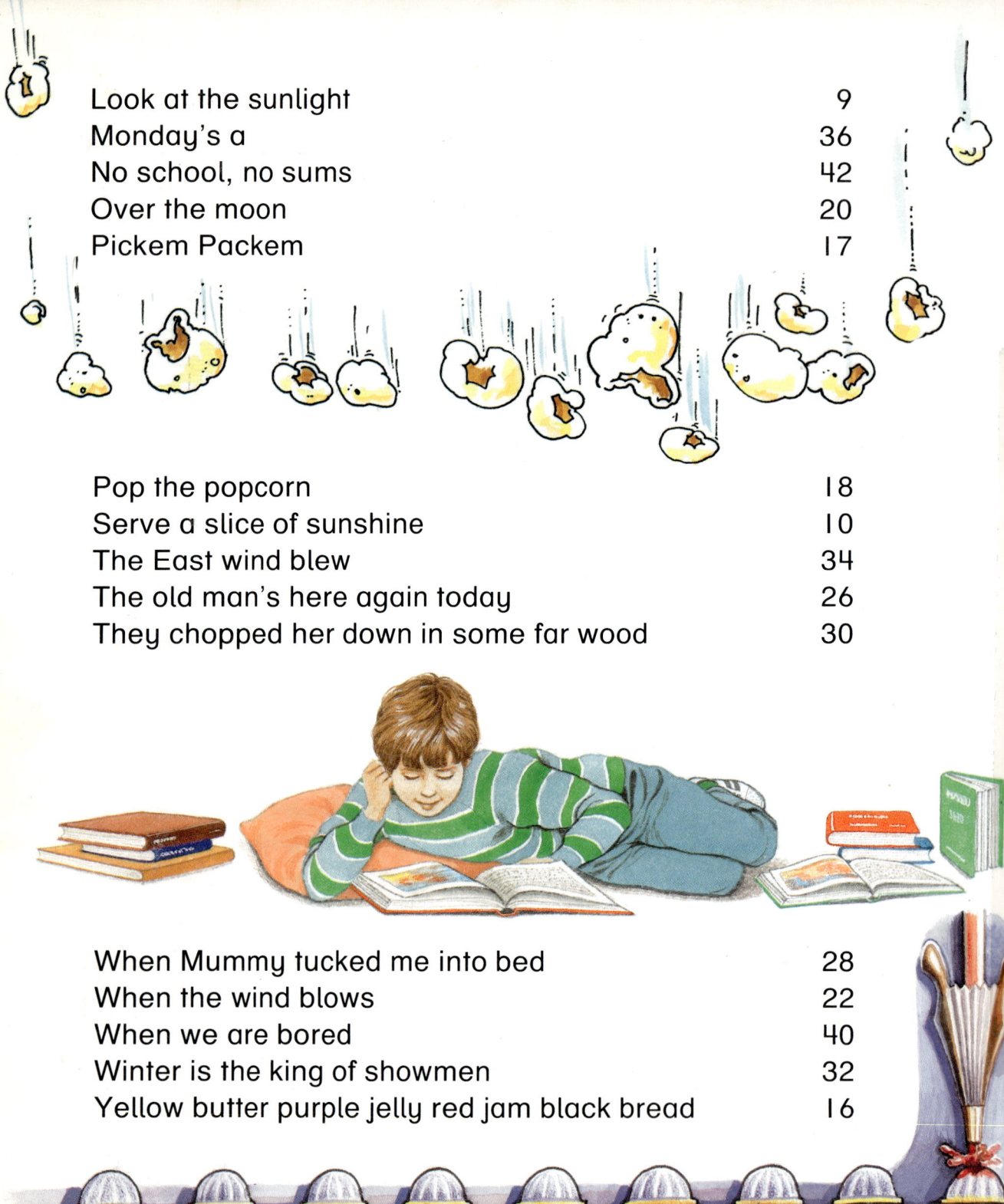